South Arbor Charter Academy
Media Center
Ypsilanti, MI 48197

Powerful Machines

Airplanes

Andrea Rivera

abdopublishing.com

Published by Abdo Zoom™, PO Box 398166, Minneapolis, Minnesota 55439. Copyright © 2017 by Abdo Consulting Group, Inc. International copyrights reserved in all countries. No part of this book may be reproduced in any form without written permission from the publisher. Abdo Zoom™ is a trademark and logo of Abdo Consulting Group, Inc.

Printed in the United States of America, North Mankato, Minnesota
102016
012017

THIS BOOK CONTAINS RECYCLED MATERIALS

Cover Photo: Shutterstock Images
Interior Photos: Shutterstock Images, 1, 16–17, 21; DPVue Studio/Shutterstock Images, 4; Elena Elisseeva/iStockphoto, 5; Alex Veresovich/iStockphoto, 6; iStockphoto, 7, 9, 10–11, 18; Zern Liew/iStockphoto, 8; Library of Congress, 12, 13; Cary Kalscheuer/Shutterstock Images, 15; Chris Parypa Photography/Shutterstock Images, 19

Editor: Brienna Rossiter
Series Designer: Madeline Berger
Art Direction: Dorothy Toth

Publisher's Cataloging-in-Publication Data
Names: Rivera, Andrea, author.
Title: Airplanes / by Andrea Rivera.
Description: Minneapolis, MN : Abdo Zoom, 2017. | Series: Powerful machines | Includes bibliographical references and index.
Identifiers: LCCN 2016949155 | ISBN 9781680799453 (lib. bdg.) | ISBN 9781624025310 (ebook) | ISBN 9781624025877 (Read-to-me ebook)
Subjects: LCSH: Airplanes--Juvenile literature.
Classification: DDC 629.133/34--dc23
LC record available at http://lccn.loc.gov/2016949155

Table of Contents

Science 4

Technology. 8

Engineering 12

Art 14

Math 16

Key Stats. 20

Glossary 22

Booklinks 23

Index 24

Science

Airplanes are heavier than air. But they can fly. Their wings have a curve. This creates **lift**.

Lift pushes the airplanes up.
It allows them to stay in the air.

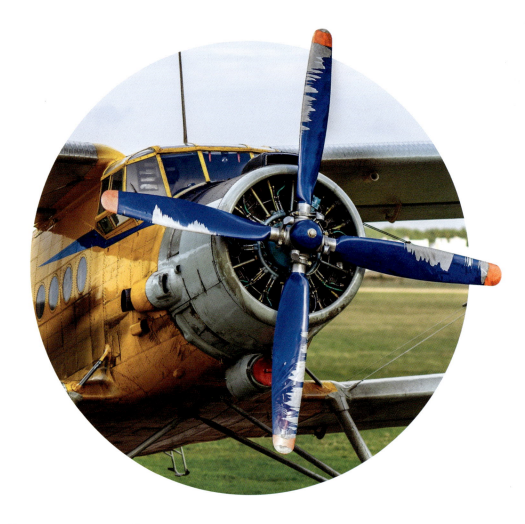

Some planes have **propellers**.

Others use **jet engines**.
They push the plane forward.

Technology

Data recorders track an airplane's information. Some track its speed or direction.

They also track how high
the plane is above the ground.

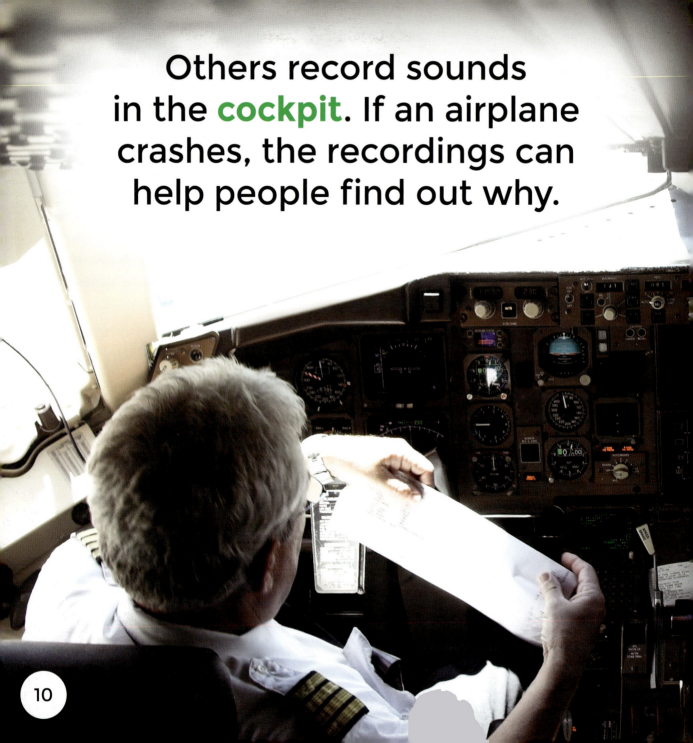

Others record sounds in the **cockpit**. If an airplane crashes, the recordings can help people find out why.

Engineering

Wilbur and Orville Wright made the first airplane.

They studied how birds flew. This helped them **design** their plane. Its wings could bend. This helped the plane steer.

Art

During World War II (1939–1945), soldiers painted pictures on their airplanes. The pictures were called nose art. Some helped identify the airplanes. Others were just for fun.

Math

Airplanes have a Mach number. It tells how fast the airplane can go.

It compares the airplane's speed to the speed of sound.

Mach 1 is the speed of sound. Some airplanes fly faster than the speed of sound. They have higher Mach numbers.

A Mach 2 airplane flies twice as fast as the speed of sound.

- The Antonov An-225 is the world's biggest airplane. It is 276 feet (84 m) long. When fully loaded, it weighs more than 1 million pounds (453,592 kg)!

- Wilbur and Orville Wright made the first airplane. They flew it on December 17, 1903.

- The Lockheed SR-71 was the fastest plane ever. It reached 2,193 miles per hour (3,530 kmh).

Glossary

cockpit - the area where the pilot sits to fly an airplane.

data - information that is collected to study or plan something.

design - to plan how something will look or be made.

jet engine - a powerful machine that shoots out hot air and gases.

lift - a force made by air flowing over and under an airplane's wings.

propeller - a device with two or more spinning blades.

Booklinks

For more information on **airplanes**, please visit booklinks.abdopublishing.com

 In on STEAM!

Learn even more with the Abdo Zoom STEAM database. Check out **abdozoom.com** for more information.

Index

cockpit, 10

data recorders, 8

jet engines, 7

lift, 4, 5

Mach number, 16, 18

nose art, 14

propellers, 6

speed, 8, 17, 18, 19

wings, 4, 13

World War II, 14

Wright, Orville, 12, 13

Wright, Wilbur, 12, 13